Matthew White

Harry Ascott Abroad

Matthew White

Harry Ascott Abroad

ISBN/EAN: 9783337122553

Printed in Europe, USA, Canada, Australia, Japan

Cover: Foto ©ninafisch / pixelio.de

More available books at **www.hansebooks.com**

HARRY ASCOTT ABROAD

BY

MATTHEW WHITE, Jr.

NEW YORK
THE AUTHORS' PUBLISHING COMPANY
BOND STREET

TO

OUR YOUNG FOLKS

AT HOME.

HARRY ASCOTT ABROAD.

CHAPTER I.

" So you're the young chap that's going to Europe all alone, are you?"

I lifted my head, for I had been hanging over the guard-rail looking down at the sea, and saw beside me a short, stout gentleman, with a very red face and a great many wraps about him. I simply replied, " Yes, sir," and waited for him to go on, as this was about the sixth time the same thing had been said to me since the steamer's departure from New York the day before.

" Europe's a big country, a very big country," continued the stout gentleman, and then he slowly shook his head, looking at me all the while in a most sympathizing manner.

" When do you think we shall reach Hamburg, sir?" I ventured to ask, hoping to stop the motion of his head, for it certainly made me feel very uncomfortable, and as if I were going to a land full of wild beasts, which would devour me with great relish immediately on my arrival.

"I don't know, I don't know," and then he began to shake his head more gravely than before, as though he expected a storm to make shipwreck of us the very next day, so I was heartily glad when he left me to myself.

Then I extended my arms along the rail again, rested my chin on my hands, my eyes on the waves, and tried to realize for the hundredth time that it was really I, Harry Ascott, of New York, fifteen years old, five feet and so many inches high, who was now on board the Hamburg steamer bound for a year's residence in that wonderful land of kings, queens, palaces, and castles called—abroad. My thoughts went back to the day when my father received a letter from an old college friend, an Englishman, whose son was at school in the little German town of Burgdorf, where the advantages were superior, the terms low, and nothing but German spoken. The writer had then gone on to say how easy it would be to put me under the care of their mutual friend, Captain Eisnach, and send me out to be educated "on the Continent."

And then I seemed to hear all over again my mother's objections, my sister's pleadings to go too, and my father's words of advice in regard to my conduct in general, and money matters in particular. And then I was on board bidding them all good-by, with Tom, Will, and John from the

Academy begging me to write often and not forget them.

Thus my mind was brought back to the sea, where my eyes were, whereupon I fell to wondering about the country to which I was going, till two bells struck, which meant one o'clock and lunch.

There were not many cabin passengers, as April was too early in the season, and those few did not particularly interest me, as they were mostly old men and young women. The captain, however, was very kind, had me sit near him at table, and frequently related long stories about the pranks he and my father and the other boy's father used to play when they were young, at which he himself would laugh immoderately; but which struck me, Young America as I was, as being rather old fogy and out of date, although, of course, I did not say so.

I had not felt at all sick thus far, and passed most of the day either looking at the sea and meditating in the manner I have described, or in learning German travelling phrases out of my guide-book, such as " Where do we change cars?" " How long do we stop here?" etc., etc. From the first I had not been a bit home-sick, on the contrary, looking forward with a great deal of pleasure and curiosity to my new home in the professor's family at Burgdorf. Then, too, I wondered not a little as to what sort of a fellow the Englishman's son would be, whether he would turn out as tip-top a lad as Tom Vintley, my chum. On these occasions I would fall to thinking about Tom, and how very far away from him I was going, when somebody would shout, "Ship a-hoy!" whereupon I would run to get my glass and try to "make her out."

Of my stout friend I did not see much after that second day out, as most of the time he was suffering the pangs unutterable in his berth, and when he did come up-stairs to sit in the little cuddy, where I sometimes retired to read, he would groan and lean his head against the side in such awful agony, that I several times feared he would die on the spot. And this reminds me that I have not yet mentioned my room-mate, a young German professor, with whom my father and the captain had quartered me, in the hope that I would thus become more accustomed to the language.

But as this poor fellow was ill the whole voyage, and as the only words I ever heard him utter were, "Ach, mein Gott! Mein Gott!" I don't see that his presence did me much good.

Thus the days wore on, each like the other, for there was no service in the cabin on Sundays as on the English steamers. Indeed Sunday was even more gay than other days, for in the afternoon the steerage passengers danced to the tune of a squeaky fiddle, while the Germans in the saloon played more games of cards and drank more wine and beer than usual.

At first this seemed very strange to me, and I thought what fit pupils they would all be for the mission schools at home ; but I am sorry to say that I soon became used to this sort of living, as Sunday on the Continent is much more of a holiday than holyday.

At length the sea voyage was over, and we steamed through the English Channel on a lovely sunshiny morning, and made our first landing at Plymouth.

Oh, how good it looked to see the green fields of England, and then the streets of the town !

"So this is Europe," I thought as I gazed toward the shore and watched the lively transfer of passengers and mail. But I did not have time to make many observations, for after a very short stop the anchor was weighed, the sails unfurled to a fair breeze, and under a full press of canvas and steam we went on our way across the Channel to Cherbourg in France, which place, however, as we called there in the night, I did not see.

While we lay at Plymouth both the stout gentleman and the young professor appeared on deck, each seeming quite cheerful and recovered ; but as soon as we left port they quickly disappeared, and on going to bed I heard my room-mate muttering over those three words again.

The next morning when I got up I found we had passed through the Straits of Dover and were in the North Sea or German Ocean, which piece of water, on that day at least, was by no means a smooth one. Indeed, when we were off the Scilly Islands, where the Schiller was lost, the ship gave such lurches and creakings, groanings and strainings, that the only lady who was able to leave her room sprang up from the dinner table, screamed, fainted away, and being placed upon one of the sofas was immediately rolled off again by a sudden pitch of the vessel, and for a time there was great commotion in the cabin.

The storm subsided during the night, and the next morning the ship entered the river Elbe, and steamed up to Hamburg through a dense fog.

And now what a busy time there was on board. The donkey engine was set to work hauling up trunks from the hold, everybody put on his best hat and clothes, while the stout gentleman and the professor seemed like two different beings. It did not take me long to gather my things together, fee the stewards according to the captain's directions, secure my money about my person, and single out my trunk from the pile. These things being attended to, I took my place by the pilot-house, and peered forward eagerly to catch the first glimpse of the city.

At last, about two in the afternoon, I began to make out a forest of masts through the fog, and in half an hour the ship came quietly up to the landing stage. As Hamburg is what they call a free city there is no custom house to pass through on arrival there, although the baggage of persons leaving by the different railroads must be submitted for examination at the several stations; thus I was enabled to quit the steamer at once and go to the hotel which the captain had selected for me.

Immediately on the vessel's being made fast, a number of men came on board to take away the luggage, and one of these, who to my great joy I heard talking English, I engaged to transport my trunk. Then I went down the gang plank, and for the first time set my foot on European soil.

The next thing was to find a cab, and seeing a number of them standing round, I went up to one of the drivers, but he muttered something in his queer jargon which sounded like "nit fry," and pointed with his whip to another carriage, which I had purposely avoided as the horse seemed ready to fall upon its knees and the man did not have a very benevolent expression of countenance. However, there was no help for it, so I marched boldly up to him, shouted out the name of my hotel as though he were deaf, and then sprang into the cab with my bag, while he slowly mounted the box.

CHAPTER II.

OF course during the ride I did nothing but look out of the window, and at first I confess I was a little disappointed in the appearance of things, for the streets through which we drove seemed pretty much like those in New York. But before long I began to think I must have made a mistake, and landed in Venice instead of at Hamburg, for there were canals on all sides, and every moment or two I caught glimpses of large sheets of water. Perhaps this was the reason there were so many people in the "dry street," as I named the one we were in, for the sidewalks were crowded on both sides, and although I tried hard to discover something queer about the inhabitants, they all looked and walked just as Americans did at home.

The stores were large and handsome, and several times I felt like stopping my driver—if I had only known how to do it—in order to have a good look in some of the windows. But we had now turned a corner, and skirting the edge of a pond, lake, or river (for during my whole stay in the city I never could exactly settle in my mind what sort of a body of water it really was), the next moment the driver pulled up his horse, which had gone along more steadily than I had thought it capable of doing even in its days of colthood, and we were standing before the hotel.

A man with a broad gilt band around his cap, who had been looking through the glass doors, instantly rang a great bell, rushed down the steps, and was immediately followed by three or four waiters, the clerk, and a porter. I got out, looking as important as I knew how, and paid the driver (the captain had counted out for me the exact fare), while the three waiters were trying to carry off my bag, of which I kept a tight hold as it contained not a few of what I considered my most precious possessions. I then walked into the house, followed by a solemn procession of the above-named individuals.

"*Ein Zimmer!*" I said to the clerk in rather a loud voice, as soon as we were within doors.

"Show the gentleman to No. 82," he replied in admirable English, addressing the man of the gilt band.

Alas for my two German words, which I had spent so much time and pains in learning! I had pronounced the latter of them with a hopeless hissing accent, which at once betrayed me. From that humiliating moment till I really could talk tolerably well, I gave up all claims to a knowledge of the "stuff," which in my disgust I then termed it.

I meekly followed the man with the key up several flights of stairs to a little room, the window of which looked out upon another nameless body of water just below. As he turned to go, he of the gilt cap stopped and said in a strange voice, as though every word he spoke in English were a stolen one: "Will you come to *table d'hôte* at four?"

I thought over the captain's directions a moment till I came to the words *table d'hôte*, and then told him yes, although I was strongly tempted to say *ja*, of which I felt sure. Thereupon I was left alone, and for the first five or ten minutes I did feel that I was alone in every sense of the word. Perhaps the weather had something to do with this, and indeed it was a most dismal day; but pretty soon curiosity got the better of any more tender feeling, and having taken a few necessary articles from my bag, I went to the window to view my surroundings.

Almost beneath my room was a handsome bridge, which was crossed continually by queer-looking omnibuses with seats running lengthwise on top, and a conductor standing on the step behind, cabs by the hundred, and now and then by a private carriage. But whichever way I turned my eyes there was a cab, and if they were not being driven hither and thither, they were standing in a long line, one behind another, waiting to be engaged.

Looking across the water to my right, I saw a

large open square that seemed to be the terminus for numerous lines of horse-cars. A ride on one of these I set down as an expedition for the morrow, for I was not to leave for Burgdorf till the evening of the day following my arrival at Hamburg. In the midst of my plan-making a great gong sounded, and I went down stairs feeling very curious in regard to my first *table d'hôte.*

I soon found the dining-room, and was shown to my seat at a long table by one of the waiters who had endeavored to get hold of my bag. There was not a lady present, and each one of the gentlemen appeared as solemn as though he were lunching at a funeral. I looked around to see if there were no passengers from the steamer among the guests; but no, there was not a familiar face in the room. As all were served with the same things, no orders were given, and if it had not been for the rattling of the knives and forks, the silence in that great dining-hall would have been something awful. Dessert over, candles were placed on the tables, at which the gentlemen lighted their cigars, and the room was soon filled with smoke.

I have forgotten to mention that before I came down, a waiter appeared with a little slip of printed paper, which I was required to fill up with my name, native place, and profession. As I modestly wrote "student" under the latter head I wondered they did not want my age too. The next day I was much gratified by seeing all this about me printed in the morning paper among the lists of arrivals.

The captain was to call at six, and as it was after five when that melancholy dinner was over, I had only time to take a short stroll under the arcades, which formed the ground floor of the hotel, and which I should think were quite a necessity in that land of fogs and rain.

On my return I got into conversation with the man of the gilt band, and while talking with him, I noticed how different the hotel was from ours in America. There was no bar-room—although what they called a beer-tunnel did a flourishing business in the cellar—no elevator, and no news, cigar, or photograph stands, nor knots of gentlemen standing round. Every thing was as quiet and orderly as in a private boarding-house, and I missed the bustle of our own hotel life not a little.

Shortly after six the captain arrived, and drawing me into the reading-room, questioned me as to how I liked Europe, Hamburg, and the house. As my experience had been rather limited except as to the last, I replied that I thought it a very nice place, which answer in my opinion covered the whole subject.

He then inquired how I got along with the German money, and if I still remembered that a mark was *about* twenty-five cents, and a pfennig *about* the fourth of one cent. On my answering these questions affirmatively, he seemed puzzled for a moment as to what he should say next, for he had no sons of his own, and although he was very lively on shipboard, he appeared to feel quite depressed and out of place on shore. At least this is what I then thought must be the matter with him, and that he was really sea-sick, or, in other words, homesick for the sea.

Suddenly his face brightened, and clapping me on the shoulder with quite a deal of violence, he burst out with: " Harry, my boy, what do you say to my taking you to the theatre?"

Now, as I had been for the three years previous at a country boarding school, it may readily be imagined that there had not presented themselves many opportunities of my attending theatrical performances, and as I was as much of a boy as any of my readers, "going to the theatre" seemed to me the very summit of all joys. I speedily signified my readiness to accompany the captain, gratefully thanking him for his munificence; and as plays in Germany begin and finish early, we were soon on our way.

As we walked along by the side of the lake, or whatever it was, my companion informed me that the theatre in the Fatherland, as he called it, was a very different thing from places of amusement in New York; that in Germany it was an educational institution, etc., etc., to all of which I am afraid I did not listen as attentively as I should, my mind being full of the wonders I was about to behold, and my eyes occupied in gazing around me.

CHAPTER III.

It was not far to the theatre, and the captain having procured good seats in the balcony, I followed him up the stairs as though my home was just across the way, and not over the trackless waste of waters, so light was my heart.

As it was not yet seven, I had an opportunity to look around me before the curtain rose, and the first thing that took my eye were the handsome uniforms of the officers in the parquet, who, with most of the other gentlemen there, stood up with their backs to the stage and surveyed the house. With the aid of the captain's opera glass, I presently discovered a youth of about eighteen, with light hair and frank blue eyes, who was standing beside a young officer in blue and white. I liked this fellow's looks immensely, and I suppose took an especial interest in him, as I had not spoken to a boy since leaving New York two weeks before. But at that moment the overture began and everybody sat down.

The opera—for in Germany they give opera as often and as cheaply as we do plays—was the *Queen of Sheba*, and such elegant scenery and magnificent costumes I know I never saw before, and I am not sure that I have since. To the music and singing I did not pay much attention, for as the captain remarked, I was not yet "educated up to it."

Between the acts every one went out and walked in a handsome hall with a waxed floor called the *foyer*, and here I saw my friend of the light hair again, at the same time observing that the soldier in blue also wore boots topped with white braid, and a very pretty cap, which together with his dangling sword gave him quite a dashing appearance. On asking the captain, I learned that he was a hussar, and also that the Prussian or German army was the greatest in the world, together with a great many other facts concerning it which I will not set down here.

The performance was over shortly before ten, and an hour later I was in my bed at the hotel, dreaming of Solomon and top-boots.

The next morning, after an eight o'clock breakfast of coffee and rolls, which is all a German or Frenchman takes at that early hour, I walked out with my red covered guide-book under my arm to see what I could of the city till noon, when the captain was to lunch at the hotel, and afterwards take me to the Zoological Gardens.

Well, I did a great deal of walking those first two hours, stopped many times in the street in order to consult my map and find out my whereabouts, and as the result of all this I remember the St. Nicholas Church with its extremely high steeple, a queer street full of water and little boats, with no sidewalks but plenty of bridges, and lastly some very pretty public gardens laid out on a sort of isthmus separating two great lakes.

It being now nearly eleven, I thought I had better take my horse-car trip, so hastening to the square already mentioned, I mounted to an outside seat on top of one of them, for in this respect they are built like the omnibuses. After we had gone a little way I laughed right out, for each time before we came to a crossing the driver rang a bell to let people know he was coming, as if the car were a locomotive going at full speed.

"Why don't they put bells on the horses?" I asked myself as the loud ding-dong, ding-dong broke out again.

However, my face sobered down very suddenly when the conductor came along for the fares.

"How much?" I asked, remembering my experience in German at the hotel. But in this case the man went through a most complicated series of gestures, from which, and the utterly stupid expression his face assumed, I concluded he had not understood me; yet rack my brain as I would, I could not think of the German phrase, while to increase my confusion and bewilderment all the other passengers began explaining to me in that same awful gibberish. At length in desperation I gave the fellow a mark, trusting to his honesty to return me the right change.

This little ceremony over, I returned to the enjoyment of the ride, for it was quite novel as well as agreeable to sit there on top and have such a fine view of every thing. As we passed a large public building, I thought I recognized a familiar form standing in front of it, and before we turned the corner I had a full view of my steamer friend, the stout gentleman, turning over the leaves of his guide-book in a most despairing manner.

And still the car went on and on, till I began to wonder whether the track was not laid in the form of a circle. However, I was determined to see the end of it, and thought that every turn would prove the last. We were now out of the city proper, in the midst of pretty country-houses surrounded by handsome gardens, and at length when it had grown to be after half-past eleven, and I was wondering what the captain would think at not finding me on time, the car halted in what seemed to be a sort of village, and then began the return trip. Just as I got off at the square, at twenty minutes past twelve, the rain, which had been threatening all the morning, began to descend, and as I made a dash for the hotel

I inwardly resolved never again to explore a city by tramway.

I found the captain waiting for me, and was profuse in my apologies for being late, which he accepted with that great good-nature for which I so highly esteemed him.

Lunch over, a cab was called, and each armed with an umbrella, we started out to "do" the Zoo Gardens, which are very similar to the grounds immediately around the arsenal in Central Park, except that an admission fee is charged. If I do not recollect all the different sorts of beasts, birds, and fishes I saw there, I do remember that it was a royally muddy place, and that the captain and I were obliged to jump about from one dry spot to another like two frogs.

"Now you must write home and tell them your opinion of Deutschland," said Herr Eisnach, when we were once more seated in the reading-room, and thereupon he procured for me an immense sheet of paper, ornamented at the top with a truthful representation of the hotel, together with the neighboring waters. As I glanced up at this picture, after finishing the first page, I could not help but think that were I not to be more than a hundred miles from Hamburg by the time the letter would reach New York, my mother would be dreadfully worried for fear I should walk in my sleep and jump into the canal under my window, which latter the captain desired me to mark for her especial edification.

Eight o'clock that evening found us at the railroad station, where I was obliged to have my bag and trunk examined by the custom-house officials. This was not at all such a terrible operation as I had imagined, and I paid the two cents on my three lemons very cheerfully.

"Good-by, Harry," said the captain, when he left me at the cars; "be a good boy, learn well, keep a brave heart, and don't forget that you change at Schnellburg and Langsamden."

I promised to remember, and was about to ask him for the third or fourth time what "how much" was in German, when the whistle shrieked; he wrung me heartily by the hand, and as he stepped down somebody else stepped up, and the next instant I found myself sitting opposite the young fellow I had noticed in the theatre.

CHAPTER IV.

"How queer!" I thought, and then as there was nobody there to introduce us, and as, if there had been, we could not in all probability have carried on a very brisk conversation unless it might be by signs, I turned to the window and flattened my nose against the pane to look down at the Elbe rolling on in the darkness under the handsome new bridge we were crossing.

Perhaps, it may seem strange to my readers that I took my first journey in a foreign country at night; but the fact was that that was the only time when I could make the connections, for Burgdorf was not on any of the main lines, which made it rather difficult of access from a distance. As there were no sleeping cars on the road, my father had thought it best for me to travel first class, in spite of the continental saying which affirms that only fools and Americans do so. I would thus have more room to stretch myself along the seats, and might perhaps avoid being shut up at midnight with a madman.

As almost every one knows, the cars in Europe are like three old-fashioned stage-coaches joined together, and are not called cars at all, but carriages.

The light was furnished by a sickly lamp let in from the roof, which in my opinion gave the compartment a much more dismal aspect than if there had been no light whatever.

Although it was April, the night air felt decidedly cool, and I lay back in my corner, bundled up in a winter overcoat, trying to imagine my feet were warm. Every once in a while I looked over at my companion, who in a great ulster and rug occupied the other end of the opposite seat.

"Pshaw!" thought I, "if this were only America we'd soon be having a jolly chat together, and if it wasn't for those ancients wanting to build the Tower of Babel—"

"Will you please take half of my rug? It is big enough for three."

I was so surprised I started up and said right out: "Hello, do you speak English? I thought you were German."

"So I am," returned the "other fellow," standing up and spreading out his rug. "But my mother was English, and we speak both at home." I felt like saying "You're a trump;" but not being sure whether or not he could fully appreciate the American heartiness of the expression, I thanked him instead for his kind offer, and went over to his side of the compartment, where, having securely done ourselves up in the robe, any one to look at us might have thought we had known one another all our days.

"How did you know I wasn't a German?" was my first question after we had tucked ourselves in all round.

"I knew you were neither German, English, nor French, but an American, because you had no rug;" and then my new acquaintance proceeded to explain that in Europe nobody travelled without one, as the cars were not heated as they are in the United States.

"Have you ever been to America?" I asked, finding this lad a queer although interesting companion, for he had a way of saying boyish things in a sort of grown-up manner that I afterwards discovered was not uncommon in his country.

"No," he replied, "nor never to England, although I'm nearly eighteen. You see I've been at the Commercial College in Hamburg for the last three or four years, and so have not had much chance to travel."

Charmed by his frankness, I at once began to tell all about myself, where I was going, why I had come, and how I had seen him the night before at the theatre.

"Why, I live at Burgdorf, and know Professor Lehren and his family quite well. I think you'll like it there, and Rudolph is a good fellow."

Upon this I was more pleased than ever, and asked a hundred questions about the town, the house, the professor, and as to who Rudolph was.

"He's the professor's son, sixteen, and speaks English and French very well."

"Whew!" I thought; "it seems I'm to be the youngest of them all. Wonder how old that English fellow Starleigh is?" and then I fell to discussing him with my Burgdorf friend, who likewise had not seen the new student, and in surmising what he would be like, tall or short, a "good fellow" or a "regular prig," we grew better acquainted than was possible by any other means.

"Hanover!" somebody cried, as the train came to a halt, and the guard opened the door to look at our tickets. I was for getting out to see what I could of the city in the dark and from the station; but as my companion informed me that it was quite away from the depôt, I remained where I was, quite content with having a boy-guide in place of a printed one in red covers.

In a few minutes the train started off again, and we two talked about everything in general, and our native countries in particular, till we both grew sleepy, and were each going off into a nice nap, when the cars stopped once more, and the conductor shouted, "Schnellburg!" "*Wagen wechsel*," murmured my neighbor, half sleep, and the words at once recalled to me my studies on the steamer, for they meant " change cars."

This was not a very pleasant thing to do in the small hours of the night, and to make matters worse we were obliged to wait ten or fifteen minutes on the platform of a little country station before the other train backed up. However, once settled in our new compartment in the old position, and with the agreeable thought that we should not have to change again till morning, we were soon in the land of nod, and I have no doubt were just about to enjoy pleasant dreams, when the cars halted at a junction, and the door on our side was opened, letting in at the same time a cold draft of air and an old gentleman.

"Here's a go, ' I whispered to my companion, as we were both thoroughly waked up by a gust of wind, and the tripping of the newcomer over our toes.

The door being shut and the engine off again, we made up for his awakening us by watching the new passenger's movements. He had a great number of wraps, which he continually arranged and rearranged about him, and when he thought all was snugly tucked in, he would pick up the little satchel by his side, and having extracted from it a small flask, he would drink therefrom and then smack his lips with great satisfaction. But before long his head began to sink lower and lower towards his breast, and then, when his chin was almost touching his great-coat, he would suddenly seem to recollect something he wanted to think about before going to sleep, whereupon he would sit bolt upright again with such a jerk that once or twice I nearly laughed out, so that at last whenever I saw his head begin the downward trip I was obliged to stuff my mouth with my comforter. However, by and by he went off to sleep in good earnest, and then such snoring! It was awful, especially since we were each trying to follow our aged friend's example, which we at length succeeded in doing, and were conscious of nothing till "*Wagen wechsel!*" again rung in our ears, and by the daylight which six o'clock furnished we left the old gentleman alone, and once more had a compartment to ourselves.

At seven we stopped half an hour for breakfast, which was a pleasing contrast to our "ten-minutes-for-refreshments" way of doing things at home. After this meal the journey proved much pleasanter, for the sun came out and warmed us both into feeling an interest in the objects along the road.

"There's the Wartburg!" suddenly exclaimed my fellow-passenger, and he pointed to a high hill on the left thickly covered with trees.

"What's that?" I asked.

He said, "Why, haven't you ever heard

Wagner's opera of "Tannhäuser?" And then I really thought it was time to make known the fact that in my country boys could talk all day about base-ball or games of any sort ; but as for opera, why that was like—like—well, they didn't know any thing at all about it, I ended up, becoming rather confused in my efforts to think of something with which to compare the classical luxury. When I had finished, my new acquaintance kindly proceeded to enlighten me in regard to the works of "the great masters ;" but I did not kindle with sympathetic enthusiasm as he talked, and was very glad when the train whizzed by a parade ground where some troops were exercising.

"Look quick!" I exclaimed, myself hanging half out of window, in order to behold as long as possible the glittering of the helmets in the sunshine. "I wonder what sort of a celebration's going on here?"

"Oh, it's no celebration at all. That great long building is the barracks, and the soldiers are only going through their daily drill."

I then recollected what the captain had told me about the immense standing army the country supported, and this brought to my mind the handsome blue uniforms I had noticed in the theatre.

"You know a great many officers, don't you?" I ventured to ask.

"Quite a number," was the reply. "My brother

is a hussar, and in a year or so, I too must be a soldier; for in Germany, as in France, every male, unless he is ill or deformed, must serve, as it is called, for at least two years."

This was by far the most startling piece of information I had yet learned, and I discussed the subject with great animation till my thoughts were turned into a new channel by discovering that it was almost time we were due at Burgdorf.

"Is this it?" I inquired with some trepidation, as the train rounded a curve, and the whistle blew for a dismal collection of stone houses, high red roofs, pig-pens, and women hoeing in the fields.

"Heaven forbid!" was the response, which I afterwards learned was the literal translation of a much-used German phrase. I drew a long breath of relief, and waited five minutes before stretching out my neck again.

"There's the fortress!" cried my companion the next moment.

"Where, where?" I exclaimed, bobbing in and out, and thereby nearly losing my cap.

"There, on that hill;" whereupon I looked and saw, off in the distance, standing proudly on its lofty elevation, what appeared to be a real, old European castle, with its towers and turrets, for all the world like those I had read about in fairy tales.

"And is that Burgdorf?" I asked, pointing to

quite a respectable assemblage of the inevitable red roofs, three or four church steeples, with a soldiers' barracks on the outskirts, the whole lying in a very pretty valley through which wound a small stream and the railway.

"Yes, here we are," and with my heart thumping violently under my coats, I got down my bag and helped my friend pack up his rug, all the while trying to look on both sides at once. As the train slowed up at the platform of the large stone station, my companion, who with his hand on the door-latch had suddenly become as eager as myself, shouted in my ear: "There they are!" and then sprang out to jump into a carriage that was waiting, and drive off.

I was so astounded at this sudden desertion, that I had almost forgotten to get out myself, when a young fellow of middling height, with light blue eyes, and an expression of perfect good-nature on his otherwise rather plain face, came up to the car-window, and with an accent so thoroughly English that there was no mistaking it, asked: "I say, aren't you the new chap coming to Professor Lehren's?"

CHAPTER V.

I WAS so glad to hear my own language spoken by one to whom it was natural, that I bounded out of the car in an instant, with a most emphatic: "Yes, I am!"

Starleigh—for it was he—insisted upon taking my bag, and then presented me in due form to the Herr Professor, a tall, bearded man, with glasses, who seemed afraid to say much in English lest he should make a mistake.

"Where's the number for your trunk, Ascott?" broke in Starleigh, and as I handed the young Englishman the slip of paper which there answers for a check, I saw at once that ours was to be a very pleasant friendship.

The express business having been arranged, and my trunk mounted on a small cart drawn by a street porter, we started to walk to the house. When the professor, after three or four false starts, had succeeded in inquiring after the health of my family, and with a half sigh of relief relapsed into silence, Starleigh, who had taken me by the arm in the most friendly manner, began to ply me with all sorts of questions, such as whether I was homesick or had been sea-sick, how much German I knew, and what I thought of the country.

It was not far to the Lehren mansion, and the large, queer-shaped house was soon pointed out to me. It was on the corner, and the streets running by it were almost narrow enough to be called alleys in America; as to what the materials were out of which it was constructed I was never quite certain, and when we entered the long, stone passage-way on the ground floor, my heart sank within me.

"Into what sort of a place am I going?" I thought.

We went up two pair of uncarpeted stairs, and then turning in at another door, I found myself in what was neither a room nor a hall, being a part of the house seemingly intended as a sort of considering-spot, where one might have plenty of space to decide which of the numerous doors and passages he would enter. But we were not given an opportunity of reflecting, for it was here that a short, cheerful-looking lady met us, who shook me warmly by the hand, and whose kindly smile fully expressed all that her tongue was not able to tell me, for Frau Lehren could not speak a word of English. And now I was formally turned over to the care of Starleigh, who confided to me on the way to our rooms that he'd been dreadfully lonesome, and was mighty glad I'd come. He led me through a narrow hallway looking out upon a little court in the centre of the building, and opening a door near the end of it, said : "Here's your drawing room, and through there's mine ;" the "through there," referring to a smaller apartment, uncarpeted, and containing a bed, wash stand, and chair multiplied by two.

"That's where we sleep," exclaimed my guide.

I stood still for a moment in my "drawing room" in a sort of horror, looking from the painted floor, with its strips of rag-carpet like islands scattered here and there, to the baby-house stove in the corner that was doing its best to give forth a little heat, then at the bare table, bureau, and the three wooden chairs, and lastly out of the window upon the narrow street, minus sidewalk, below.

"How different from—" I began to soliloquize, when Starleigh's cheery voice called me to come and see his room, where he had gone to poke up the fire.

The apartment corresponded exactly with mine in its primary elements, and yet how different it appeared ! On the table was a bright red cloth, covered with books and writing materials, the walls were adorned with pictures cut out of old newspapers, and depicting all sorts of scenes from the Bridge of Sighs to an organ grinder's monkey, while here and there were displayed some amateur attempts at painting.

"We'll soon furnish you up," said this most cheerful of mortals, and then he told me how his room had been as bare as mine at first, and how he had made it what it was out of mere scraps from his trunk.

"Dinner will be ready soon," he concluded, "and afterwards we'll go out and I'll show you the sights of Burgdorf."

So I took heart again and began unpacking. Little did I imagine then how attached I was to become to the old house and to that barren little room!

While I was brushing my hair the bell rang, and in a few minutes I was ushered into the eating-room, as it is called in German.

The floor was painted brown, as they were all through the building, and at one end was a piano, at which was seated when we entered a lad with a bright face and curly hair. Starleigh introduced him as Rudolph, and then we all sat down to table, which I must say was a most bountiful one, affording not the slightest hint of *sauerkraut*.

My introduction to Rudolph brought to mind my unknown friend of the railroad journey, whom I had completely forgotten in the excitement attending my arrival. Upon my description of him, the son of the house informed me in his pretty good English that my chance acquaintance was none other than the young Von Rothstall, whose brother was a baron, and who in consequence considered himself as much superior to the other youths of the town.

"But he said you were a good fellow!" replied I innocently.

"Did he?" returned the other; and ceased at once his attacks on the young Von's haughtiness.

I will not deny that I felt rather pleased to think that I had been on such intimate terms with a baron's brother, and in my next letter home wrote about him in grand style, although I was careful not to mention the abrupt manner in which our acquaintance had terminated.

"Now for seeing the sights!" exclaimed Starleigh, when, dinner over, the professor and his wife retired to nap till coffee at two, as is the custom of the country. "Will you come, Rudolph?"

The latter declined in German, and as we went down-stairs Starleigh explained to me that he, Rudolph, was in the highest class at the Gymnasium—a school were one is prepared for the universities—and consequently was obliged to do a deal of studying.

"There goes one of the students now," he added, as we reached the street; and I saw a fellow with a most ridiculously small green cap atop of his head.

"The boys in the other school wear black caps

with silver braid," explained my new guide-book boy. "But here we are in the market-place."

This was a large square, with all sorts of old fashioned buildings facing on it.

"Just wait till Saturday," said Starleigh; "the big market is held here then, and such a sight as it is! Old *Fraus* with great baskets of butter strapped to their backs, crockery of all shapes, sorts, and sizes spread out in the street, and oh, such an odor of frying sausages! But now let's take a look at the Court Garden;" and then we went through some more narrow streets, with still narrower sidewalks, and oftener no sidewalks at all. After turning two or three corners we came out upon a handsome square, from whence I obtained a glimpse of the old fortress.

"Can't we go up to it?" I asked, all impatience to behold the moat, cross the drawbridge, and climb upon one of the turrets.

"Yes, but not now, for we must go back to coffee pretty soon. See, there's the palace, and opposite is the Court Theatre; and, yes, how jolly, here comes the Duke himself, driving with the Duchess!"

And sure enough at this moment a carriage issued from the portal of the castle and came towards us.

"Now you must make your best bow; but be sure and take a good look at him, for he's nearly related to the British throne," directed Starleigh, and as the carriage rolled by within a few feet of us we both doffed our caps with our politest air.

To my great astonishment and delight his Highness gravely returned the salute, while the Duchess slightly inclined her head. I was quite awe struck for a minute or two, not from any thing about the turn-out itself, or in the appearance of the occupants, but simply because I had seen and had had a bow from nobility.

We returned to the professor's by way of the principal street, which was every bit as queer-looking and old fashioned as any of the others, only with more stores on it, or "shops," as Starleigh called them. We had by this time grown quite confidential, and were already making plans for the jolly times we'd have going around together when I had learned somewhat of the language.

"Is it very hard?" I asked in some anxiety.

"It's more mixed up with cases and genders and such things than French is. You know French, don't you?"

I was obliged to confess my ignorance of the tongue, at the same time regarding Starleigh with more respect, as I added: "Where did you learn it?"

"Oh, we all study it in England; but I see now you Americans, being off there by yourselves, don't need it as much as we do, with only the Channel between us. But you'll soon learn German, although at first it seems rather slow work, for the professor makes you write the letters over and over again before he teaches you another thing. By the by, there's to be a concert to-morrow night at Frieden's Garden; we'll go, and I'll show you some of the natives at their best."

After coffee Starleigh and I accompanied Herr and Frau Lehren to the fortress. The way lay through the beautiful Court Garden, which was open to every one, and on reaching our destination my anticipations were fulfilled in every particular. There was the moat, now laid out as a promenade, and crossing it was the bridge, which, however, was a stone one, and at the top of the gateway that gave entrance to the interior was a most interesting row of long iron spikes, ready to pounce down upon the first enemy that came along. However, notwithstanding their interesting nature, I was glad when I had passed them. Here, after having had a most glorious view of all the surrounding country—obtained from a little platform extending out from the lofty walls—we had coffee again, partaking of it, in company with some others at little tables set out under the trees within the inclosure.

This struck me as a most delightful way of spending the afternoon, and I asked Starleigh if the family often came up there for coffee and cake.

"About once a week," he replied; "and there are plenty of other nice places to go to besides."

My lessons were to begin the following morning, and at the supper table I learned the German for knife, spoon, fork, etc., after which Rudolph played on the piano and Frau Lehren sang. Altogether the evening passed away in quite a home-like fashion, and when we had gone to bed, Starleigh and I lay awake and talked for some time about young Von Rothstall, who I affirmed was a very jolly fellow in spite of his title.

CHAPTER VI.

I WILL not stop to describe my first steps in the new language, the pains the good professor took with me, nor our long walks in the fields and woods together, during which he taught in the pleasantest manner the names of trees, streams, and flowers. I will only say, that living in a constant atmosphere of German as I did, and with the desire to know as much as Starleigh—who had had three months the start of me—to spur me on, it did not require as much time as I had anticipated till I could talk a little and understand a great deal. Even those first weeks of hard study were very pleasant ones, what with the lovely spring weather, the merry pic-nics, the garden concerts, and now and then a visit to the theatre. But I must pass over this period and bring my story up to the middle of July, when Starleigh and I began our famous tour.

Our friendship had grown firmer with every month, and as Rudolph was busy with his studies, and my friend the baron's brother had left town again shortly after my arrival, we were always together. Indeed, if it had not been that we could talk to one another, I believe we would have almost forgotten our own language.

One evening in the latter part of May, as we were enjoying the music of the military band in one of the gardens, Starleigh suddenly burst out with: "I say, Ascott" (it is a peculiarity of English fellows, no matter what chums they may be, to always call one another by their last names), "what shall we do during vacation? You know it lasts a month, from the middle of July, and oh my! wouldn't it be jolly for you and I to go off on a trip somewhere?"

"Jolly!" I replied. "I should say it would. But where could we go, and," in a very doubtful tone, "how?"

"Write home for leave and money. It would be a capital thing for us, exercise our German, give us experience, and really make men of us," he concluded laughingly.

Thus the project was set on foot, two pleading letters were forthwith dispatched to four indulgent parents, and by return of post came the desired permission, coupled with maternal warnings to be careful, and not to forget our light overcoats. As Starleigh naturally heard from home before it was possible that I could, I passed three weeks in terrible suspense, during which my friend tried his best to keep up my spirits by vowing he would not go a mile without me.

This devotion touched me deeply, and in return for it I inwardly determined not to say a word about celebrating the Fourth of July, for fear of offending his loyal British feelings. When my reply arrived, and we had added up our funds, the important question again arose as to where we should go.

"Down the Rhine," I suggested, as one hot afternoon we sat in my "drawing room," with our letters of credit, maps, and guide-books spread out on the table before us.

"But we want to go out of Germany, to see something new," returned Starleigh, whose notions were on a much larger scale than mine. "We're in Germany now, don't you see, and it would be much jollier to start off on a regular rambling tour of the Continent. But now for the map in detail : Spain is too far, and besides we can't speak Spanish ; same fault to find with Italy. But how I would like to see just one bull-fight in Madrid ! However, here's France—"

"That's it !" I exclaimed, jumping up. "Let's go to Paris. You can do the talking part, and there's more to see there than anywhere else in the world."

"I'm a little out of practice with my French," replied Starleigh, growing red ; "besides, you know we wrote home that our trip would afford us splendid drill in German. But stop ! What a brilliant pair we are ! Here's just the place for us ; but so small that we couldn't see it," and he put his finger over Switzerland. " There they speak both French and German, there the glorious Tell was born, and thither we'll betake ourselves and plant the British flag atop of Mont Blanc !"

" The very thing," I replied, not referring to the flag in question, nor even to the mountain (for I happened to know that the latter was *not* on Swiss soil) ; but to the decision, which we finally ratified amid much enthusiasm and comparing of charges.

A few days previous, Frau Lehren had invited us to accompany herself and Rudolph to their Bad (the German for watering-place) ; but we had gratefully declined, Starleigh adding that we were bad enough already, which ingenuous pun was of course wholly lost upon the good lady. However, in making out the route which we had chosen, Rudolph rendered us not a little assistance, so arranging it that we could make a complete circle, returning to Burgdorf without going over the same road twice, and yet including all the most interesting places.

We calculated that the tour would require about two weeks, and thus we could be back in time for the annual Schuetzenfest, held the first days of August. So every thing was arranged, and we were to start the first Wednesday in vacation.

What a state of excitement we were in, to be

sure, and what a never-to-be-forgotten moment it was when we were actually off, like two young knights of the olden time going to seek their fortunes, only we were to spend money instead of making it, and were forced to put up with a snorting locomotive in place of prancing steeds. We travelled second class, were determined to talk nothing but German with railway officials and hotel clerks, and, in short, resolved to be as independent as possible.

The first place on our programme was Frankfort-on-the-Maine, and having left Burgdorf at noon we were not due there till evening. We changed cars twice, at the second junction taking our two o'clock coffee in true German style. During this journey I noticed the great precautions everywhere apparent to guard against accidents. By the side of the track ran a wire that telegraphed ahead the approach of trains, every cross road was supplied with bars or gates, flagmen there were in plenty, and at each station a sort of bell arrangement, which the cars set ringing as they arrived.

We were rather tired on reaching Frankfort, for the ride had been a long one, with not even a disagreeable fellow-passenger to break the monotony of it, and as we got into a bright yellow cab with a huge number painted on behind, we agreed that it would be wiser to divide the distances more equally, and determined to stop at Heidelberg the following day, instead of going straight through to Baden-Baden, as we had originally intended. We had selected most of our hotels before starting, either from the guide-book, or on the recommendation of Professor Lehren, who had himself been over the greater part of our proposed route. As we drove along, I noticed how clean and neat every thing looked, and what a number of large, open squares there were.

"Here we are!" exclaimed Starleigh, as the cab stopped before a building handsome as to exterior, and the interior of which I shall always remember as the most elegant of any that I saw on the Continent.

"Do be careful, Starleigh," I entreated when we had been shown to a room with lofty, frescoed ceiling, heavy curtains, and red glass pitcher and washbowl, "and don't break any thing. I wonder if our money is all safe?"

But just as we were about to count our coins and make sure our letters of credit had not taken unto themselves wings, a waiter came up with his little slips for us to register.

"Why cannot they have a book for the purpose down-stairs, as we do?" I exclaimed when he had departed, drawing forth the circular letters from under the pillow and taking my hat off the silver.

We had our tea in a most magnificent dining-hall, and not long thereafter went to bed.

"What would the Academy boys say to see me now?" I thought, as I lay under the blue silk coverlet and looked up at the gorgeous canopy overhead; and then it seemed to me that I had been away from home for years, and then that the principal and teachers of the school were chasing me over the Continent of Europe, and so I fell asleep.

We had ourselves waked very early the next morning, and as it was had just time to visit the famous Palm Garden—since burned down—with its rocks, trees, and waterfalls all under glass, and then rush off to catch the train for Heidelberg.

Both Starleigh and I became quite sentimental over this beautiful place on the banks of the winding Neckar, with the romantic ruins of its old castle on the hill above the town.

"How grand, how sublime!" spouted the young Englishman, as he stood in one of the crumbling windows, and looked out over the plain below, dotted with houses, varied by fields devoted to different crops and divided by the curving stream.

"Would the young gentlemen have the goodness to step down-stairs and view the great beer barrel?" broke in the guide, and never again during our travels did either of us venture to grow audibly enthusiastic.

The next place on our time-table was Baden-Baden, and very eagerly did both of us watch out for the first glimpse of it.

"What a pity the gambling has been abolished," quoth wicked Starleigh; "it would be such fun to hear the winning colors called out, and see them rake in the money. My, how exciting it must be!" and the fellow's eyes glistened so, that I really thought it my duty, being his senior by three weeks, to preach him a short sermon on the evils of the system, and had just reached my thirdly, when the train stopped at a pretty little station and we were there.

The place reminded me somewhat of Long Branch, the hotels being all in a line with a walk and drive in front of them, but instead of facing the ocean, a chain of hills just across the road faced them. Indeed, the town seemed to be literally faced down with hills and mountains on all sides, and when the weather is very warm—which it most decidedly was during our stay there—it seems as if the air were completely shut out. At one point the hills in front retreated a little and made room for three or four quite extensive buildings, among them the Spring House, where everybody goes to drink the waters; the Conversation House, a sort of public club; and a very pretty little theatre. By the way, it seems to me that whether towns in Germany have a church or not, it is a settled thing that they must possess a theatre.

The hotel we had chosen was opposite the Spring

House, and after dinner Starleigh and I thought we would go over and try the waters, but as we ascended the steps I suddenly bethought me that neither of us had any particular complaint of which we wished to be cured, and so we merely walked through the long building, and then wended our way to the Conversation, as it is familiarly called. And here the scene was gay enough indeed. The grounds in front of the great piazza were laid out in pleasant walks and tasteful flower beds; at one side was a handsome music pavilion and just below this stood a long, low structure, consisting of a series of shops or bazars, where the most tempting articles were exposed for sale, from simple toys at a mark to elegantly carved musical cottages from Switzerland at hundreds of thalers.

Starleigh and I wandered for quite a time among these, selecting presents which we never bought, and determining on having one thing only to allow of our eye being caught by another still more attractive. At length I broke out with: "Come, Starleigh, this won't do. You know very well we sha'n't buy any thing in the end, so what's the good of moping round the windows."

As we left this Vanity Fair and turned towards the Conversation, we noticed that the piazza of the latter was becoming rapidly filled with people, and, as soon after the band began to take possession of the music-stand, we saw that there was to be a concert.

"I don't see any gates to keep the public out. I wonder if it's a free, gratis, for nothing affair?" remarked Starleigh.

"There must be tickets to it," added I, as we followed the crowd up the steps to the porch. "See, all those around us have them;" and I began to think we had better leave before we were asked to, when a pleasant voice at my side said in English: "Excuse me, but if you'll come, I'll show you where you can obtain cards."

CHAPTER VII.

I TURNED round, and at the first glance saw that the speaker, a pleasant-looking young fellow of about eighteen, was an American. With many thanks, Starleigh and I accepted his services, and as we bought our tickets at a small desk in the entrance-way to the grand *salon*, he explained that each card was good for so many concerts, hence our having seen such a number outside with them.

We all three took chairs together, and began to talk as only strangers possessing the same language can talk, when they fall in with one another in a foreign land. Before the band struck up, we had exchanged cards, and discovered that our new acquaintance was Harvey Wintville, of New York.

"I am travelling with my father," he explained, "and to tell the truth, find it rather dull, for we've been here two weeks, on account of the waters, and I'm growing pretty tired of the place. It's lots of fun to watch the people though; they are of all nations, and such a mixture of manners, tongues, and dress can be found, I think, nowhere but in Baden."

The scene was indeed a very lively one, for the piazza was crowded with handsomely dressed ladies and gentlemen; while on the broad walk before it hundreds of couples promenaded back and forth in the gas and moonlight, and to the music of the band. So we passed the evening very pleasantly, and the following day renewed our acquaintance with young Wintville by taking a walk with him all over the town. On the latter occasion it was arranged that we three should attend the grand ball to be given the next evening in the magnificent *salons* of the Conversation House.

"But we haven't any swallow-tail coats!" objected Starleigh, when the subject was first broached.

"Oh, that doesn't matter," replied our friend. "I have an extra one, which I'll cheerfully lend to either of you who wants to dance and—"

"Oh, no; we would not dance for any thing!" we both broke in, upon which Wintville told us that he could get us in very easily in our "Sunday best," and then took us off to his hotel, where we were introduced to his father.

The result of this interview was a proposition on the part of the latter to have his son accompany us on our trip through Switzerland.

"I should like to remain here for some time yet," he explained; "but I know Harvey would not object to a change of scene, and I don't think he could do better than join your party for a while. Now, boys, what is your opinion?"

It is needless to say that both Starleigh and myself were delighted at this proposal, for we had each voted young Wintville a prime fellow, and had just been lamenting that we would be obliged to part company with him so soon, as on Monday we were to leave for Bâle.

The ball was a most brilliant affair, for all the fashionable summer-world of Baden was present, and the rooms, with their elegant conservatories and bounteous supper tables, were splendid in the extreme.

"I say, Ascott," whispered Starleigh, as we stood in a corner—did two boys of our age ever attend a grand party and *not* stand in a corner?—watching Harvey thread the mazes of the dance with a young American belle, "that was a lucky speech of yours about those tickets Thursday night. That Wintville was awfully jolly to get us in here, and I only wish I could waltz as well."

The next moment Harvey came for us and carried us off to present to his partner, whereupon we both blushed exceedingly, and both started together to remark what a very pleasant ball it was. However, it did not take us long to become better acquainted, and before the next quadrille began I had discovered that Miss Angely knew Miss Branton, who in turn knew my sister.

But as it is not the purpose of this narrative to

describe balls or young ladies, I must hasten on to other matters, merely remarking that we spent the remainder of the evening very agreeably, and on Sunday attended the English Church, where Starleigh had to find all the places in the prayer-book for me.

We three left by the noon train on Monday, with great anticipations in regard to our Swiss tour. Although Wintville did not know German, he spoke French quite fluently, and thus we were fully equipped in the language department. But whew, what a warm ride it was! The heat seemed to be concentrated in the form of a hot wind, which Starleigh declared was a simoon. To make matters worse, our compartment was full and the train crowded, so we were forced to perspire and bear it till late in the afternoon, when we reached our destination, the border town between Germany and Switzerland.

"But the conductor shouted Basel, not Bâle," objected Wintville, as we prepared to descend.

Starleigh explained that Basel was the German of it, while I took out my hotel memorandum and declared for the "Three Kings." But first we had to go through the formalities of the custom-house, which consist in the officer's asking you if you have any thing to declare, when of course you say no, whereupon he puts a chalk mark on your baggage and you walk out.

The hotel of the Three Kings—which royal personages, in gorgeous purple robes and gilded crowns, were all displayed over the main entrance—was delightfully situated on the very banks of the Rhine, which here flows quite swiftly, and just above the spot where the boat is hauled from shore to shore by means of ropes. After dinner we took a walk through the place, which, in the residence portion, seemed almost like a city of the dead, so quiet was it. Wintville, whose sentimental feelings had not received the sudden shock ours had experienced, quite raved over the terrace behind the old church. And well he might, for on looking over the stone parapet one sees the Rhine rolling by a hundred feet below, while the cathedral and the perfect stillness pervading the place render the scene doubly impressive, especially at the sunset hour.

We left for Berne early the following morning, and passed through some of the most interesting sections of the country. There were long and short tunnels, sharp curves, high mountains and deep valleys, and as the train went rushing on, the scenery became still grander. About noon we crossed the little river Aar on a lofty bridge, and the next moment the cars rolled into the station at Berne. Our hotel here was splendidly situated in terraced grounds above the river, and next door to the capitol of Switzerland.

"And now for the bears!" cried Starleigh the minute we were through lunch, and off we started for the pits, which we finally discovered after walking under low, queer arcades most of the way.

"Why, they look just like other bears!" I exclaimed, a trifle disgusted, as I gazed down at the great, ugly beasts shambling around on the stone floor. I think I must have had an idea that the Berne bears, of which I had heard so much, were gifted with the power of speech or something of that sort.

"And now let's have a look at the wonderful clock," said Wintville; so back we marched to gape at the side of a tower, where there was quite a complicated arrangement of clock-face and works and queer little figures.

Our next move was to take us among the snow mountains, and three happier lads than we were, it would be difficult to imagine, as we stood on the deck of the pretty little steamer that was to bear us across the Lake of Thun to Interlaken. We had come down by rail from Berne inside of a couple of hours, and we now had a full view of several of the highest peaks of the Bernese Oberland, as the chain is called. There was the snowy Monch, the spotless Jungfrau, and two or three others before us, while on our right and left towered barren pinnacles almost as high. The boat was crowded with tourists, and alpenstocks, with the names of ascended mountains cut into them, were to be seen on all sides. For want of time we had reluctantly given up the idea of doing any climbing ourselves, although Wintville thought of going up the Niessen—the highest of the snowless peaks—on his return.

The sail over the lake was a most delightful one. The boat touched at several places during the passage, each more prettily situated than the last, and when we reached the other end, where there was a cunning train of cars with seats on top waiting for us, the land of Tell rose to the height in our esteem that it has ever since retained.

The ride to Interlaken was much too short for us, but we were consoled as we drove along in the hotel omnibus by feasting our eyes upon that lovely mass of snow, with its silver horn, visible in the distance through an opening in the mountains, said opening forming the famous valley of Lauterbrunnen. All the hotels face this snowy maiden, while the scenery in the rear of them is scarcely less grand, for they are built along the base of a mountain towering above them to an immense altitude.

In the evening we attended a concert at the Kur Garten, an establishment kept up by the hotels, which each charge their guests ten cents a day in their bills for the use of it. We sat down at one of the little tables, ordered ice cream, which we had done at every such place on our route in the most extravagant fashion, and while we slowly allowed the fair-to-middling mixture to melt in our mouths, watched the constant stream of people, listened to the music, or gazed upon the moon illumined Jungfrau before us. I have often thought of that night since, and wished to live it over again with its— but the beer barrel recurs to my mind, and I must hasten on to more practical matters.

"I move we visit the Grindelwald Glacier to-day," proposed Wintville at the breakfast table next morning.

No sooner said than done, for in spite of the distance—several miles—we quickly hired a carriage, and before long were driving up the Valley of Lauterbrunnen—only wells—in fine style.

After passing through most charming scenery, consisting of green mountain slopes dotted with pretty little *châlets*, swift flowing streams dashing along their rocky beds, and white or brown peaks majestic in their height, the carriage left us at a small hotel still some distance from the object of our trip.

Here we took horses—and such animals as they were!—and rode over the roughest sort of country for almost an hour, when in turn we were obliged to leave even the horses and proceed the remainder of the way on foot.

And now the glacier lay before us, a great dirty-white mass of ice, running out of a sort of valley among the mountains down into the plain below. But this was not all we were to see of the thing, for there was a tunnel cut into it, to which we gained access by means of ice steps. As we entered the cavern we were almost deafened by the roar of a volume of water, which poured from some opening near the roof and ran away into the plain behind us.

The tunnel extended some little distance back into the glacier, and at the end a sort of chamber was hollowed out in which our faces had quite a ghastly appearance. This was one of the most interesting places we had yet visited, and we rode our bony beasts back uncomplainingly.

As we entered our room that night at the hotel, I saw a paper lying on the table, and thinking it might be one of the daily bills they sometimes made out, I picked it up and then gave a cry of horror. It was Starleigh's letter of credit!

"What if I had remembered its whereabouts when we were riding those old nags down that rock to the brook! But never mind, it sha'n't happen again," said our lucky friend, as he put his precious document away, and after this warning we were all particularly careful in regard to our moneyed interests. We had changed our German coin for French at

Baden, and in the comprehension of the new system Wintville was of great assistance to us.

Our next move was across the azure Lake Brienz to the famed Giessbach Falls, where we remained overnight to behold the " grand illumination," which wasn't grand at all. Then we had a glorious ride by stage-coach across the Brünig Pass to Alpnach, where we took another steamer on another lake— the one of the Four Cantons in William Tell's region —and so to Lucerne.

Here we put up at an elegant hotel, promenaded up and down the walk by the lake, and witnessed another illumination, this time a more respectable one, of Thorwaldsen's lion, carved in the side of a hill. The next day was Sunday, and for Monday was set down the grand feature of our trip, the ascent of the Rigi.

CHAPTER VIII.

To our great joy the morning of the eventful day dawned bright and clear, and long before nine we were on board the steamer that was to bear us over the lake again to Vitznau, from which point the railroad started. A great number of persons make the ascent of the mountain on foot, but as we did not feel inclined to walk to a height of five thousand nine hundred feet, and above all were curious about the railway, we had unanimously decided in favor of the latter.

There was a squeaky band of music on the boat, and forgiving the squeak, we cheerfully put some coppers into the hat which the first " violin" passed around, so elated were we at the prospect of going above the clouds.

In due time we reached the desired haven, and then what a scramble there was for the cars! These are very much like the smoking-cars on our city railroads, and the boiler of the locomotive is so placed that it shall always be level. At last every one had managed to find a seat in one of the three trains, the signal was given, and the ascent began.

Perhaps for those who have visited Mount Washington, in New Hampshire, this ride would not be much of a novelty ; but we had never been on a similar contrivance in our lives and so were considerably excited.

"But don't—you think—the motion is—rather jerky?" asked Starleigh. "It's almost—as bad as the—Channel," and indeed he did become rather pale.

But we speedily forgot all other matters in the excitement of going through a tunnel, in which we were nearly suffocated with the smoke and steam from the engine, only to emerge and cross a cobweb of a bridge suspended in mid-air half way up the mountain.

Now and then the route would curve, enabling us to obtain most lovely glimpses of the lake below glittering in the sunshine, and by and by we stopped at a place where there was a station, a large hotel, and an American flag flying, all of which appeared as if stuck on with glue to the side of the hill.

But we had not yet attained the summit, and before arriving there we passed through a cloud that enveloped us like a fog for some time. However, when at length the end was reached, where a waiter from one of the two hotels came out to ring a dinner bell for ten minutes, we made a dash for the highest point, and there gave vent to oh's and ah's of the most intense wonderment and satisfaction.

And was it not worth while to ascend to such a height, in order to be able to look down sheer four thousand four hundred feet to the lakes of Zug and Zürich, lying like bits of glass placed in " make believe" parks below us?

"There's Lucerne yonder," said Wintville, and he handed me the glass he had brought.

" I don't see any thing but clouds," I replied, giving it back.

"Why, that's queer," he returned; "it's as plain as day to me, and you looked in exactly the right direction too."

"But don't you see, " put in Starleigh, who had sharper eyes than either of us, "there are little pieces of cloud sailing between us and the town every minute or two."

And in truth this proved to be the fact, certain points being distinctly visible at one instant and completely obliterated the next. We partook of *table d'hôte* on the summit, and returned late in the afternoon, highly enthusiastic over our trip.

Of course we found plenty of people ready to tell us that we hadn't seen what was the most worth seeing, namely, the sunrise from the top; but as it rained "cats and dogs" the next morning, we could afford to take our departure for the Falls of the Rhine with a great deal of satisfaction. Truth to tell, the occasions are few and far between when shivering tourists are able to behold the king of the day burst forth in all his majesty from beneath them.

After we had ridden about an hour the rain ceased, and we all became interested in gazing out upon the ever changing landscape, when I was suddenly seized with a recollection that caused me to start up from my seat and exclaim in despairing tones:

"Oh, my journal, my journal, and my account-book too! I've left them both behind!"

This was indeed quite a serious loss, for I had prided myself not a little upon my "Diary of Foreign Travel," as I had ambitiously entitled it, and to think that it, together with the record of my outlay for creams, fruits, candy, etc., should be open to the vulgar eyes of any chambermaid or waiter who knew enough English to read them, was harrowing.

"I'd make an effort to recover the books, at any rate," suggested Harvey. "Telegraph back for them at Zürich, to be sent C. O. D. to Stuttgart. I guess the train will stop long enough."

As it turned out we would have had time to dispatch a hundred messages, for we missed a connection and were forced to wait at the Zürich station an hour. Here I sent back word to Lucerne for the hotel people to forward my possessions after me, with but little hope of ever seeing them again.

We reached Schaffhausen towards evening, but to Wintville and I, who had beheld the majesty of Niagara, the cataract of the Rhine seemed a puny one indeed.

Starleigh was very properly impressed with it, however, and in truth, if the falls are not high, they are rather picturesque, and when one looks through the stained glass windows, artfully placed near the brink, the effect is quite fine, while the roar of the waters makes a very respectable noise.

The next morning we had an unwelcome ceremony before us, and that was to take leave of Harvey, who was to return to his father at Baden, while we continued on our way back to Burgdorf, *via* Stuttgart and Nuremburg. We all rode together to the station, where we parted with much regret, and promises of frequent correspondence.

Our journey that day seemed unusually tedious and wearisome. Even the chain of queer shaped hills which we passed did not compensate us for the heat and the crowded compartment.

"Let's change to first class!" I at length exclaimed, in sheer desperation.

So as we had not spent thus far as much as we had allowed ourselves—perhaps the non-existence of soda-water in Europe may account for this fact—we called the guard, and having paid the difference, received from him numberless little tickets, which entitled us to the grandeur and solitariness of a first class coupé.

We reached Stuttgart at four, and repaired to the hotel adjoining the dépôt, which latter, by the way, is one of the handsomest on the Continent. After dinner we hired a carriage—another extravagance excused by the lack of the great American beverage—and drove through the city, which is a very pretty one indeed, many of the houses standing in the midst of the most beautiful gardens. We passed the evening at the park, where there was music by a military band.

The next day we were shown over the palace by an attendant, who rattled off his explanations at such frightful speed that neither Starleigh nor I could understand a single word, although we both looked as wise as owls, and said "ja" at what we considered the proper intervals. In one of the rooms was a large arm chair that began to play a tune as soon as you sat in it, and stopped short when you got up.

The following morning there was a knock at our door before we were dressed, and on its being opened to a crack, an important looking document was handed in, which informed me that there was a package for H. Ascott at the general post-office.

"My journal!" shouted I; and hurrying on my clothes spent nearly an hour in endeavoring to discover exactly the correct official to whom I was to apply. Finally I recovered both the books and left the city with a light heart.

The next and last stopping-place on our programme was Nuremberg ; but as it rained most persistently during our half-day's stay there, we did not see much of it except great, gloomy looking buildings, a tall church, and a few sheets of stagnant water.

And now both Starleigh and myself were eager to reach Burgdorf again, to which, in the few months of our lives passed there, we had become closely attached.

When the train arrived at noon of Saturday, and we found the professor and his wife at the station to welcome us, it did indeed seem like home after our two weeks of wandering.

And so our tour was happily ended, and we had quite a goodly sum of money left over, which we determined to expend in the enjoyments of the great bird-shooting festival, a description of which, together with sundry other matters relative to Burgdorf, will be found in the next chapter.

CHAPTER IX.

"But where are the birds?" I asked of Starleigh, as we stood on the village green in the midst of a confused mass of dirty tents, frying sausages, merry-go-rounds, and an awful crowd.

"I'm sure I don't know," he replied. "I think they must have all been shot in the early ages of this stupendous celebration. It's enough to deafen men, let alone killing smaller beings outright"

Indeed the noise was almost intolerable. Above everything else sounded the everlasting tunes of the merry-go-round organs, and as there were several of these in operation at the same time, such a babel of discords was the result as I have never since been able to forget. The shooting consisted in paying so much for a trial at knocking over a row of Punch and Judy figures, while the other entertainments, offered to the public at reasonable sums, were composed of a short fat woman, and a tall lean one, a live walrus flopping dejectedly about in a basin of water, a lively collection of educated fleas, the laughter cabinet—a booth filled with looking glasses, that gave one's countenance sundry varied and hideous aspects—and a horse that had been shot in the

Franco-Prussian war, and which, according to the showman, ought to have died then ; but, wonderful to relate, was living still, and could be seen for only ten pfennige. All of these curiosities and monstrosities, and many more besides, did Starleigh and I behold, and we ceased not to talk and laugh over them for some time afterwards.

The remainder of vacation was spent very pleasantly in taking long walks, visiting the Duke's hunting grounds, or now and then hiring a carriage and driving to one or another of the famous old churches or convents in the vicinity. Perhaps if we had been at home this sort of enjoyment would have seemed dry and tame to us, but living in a foreign atmosphere as we did, the novelty of every thing charmed us, and I now look back upon that summer as one of the brightest in my life.

The holidays over, we resumed our studies with renewed energy, and before long began to dip into the beauties of German literature. But we were scarcely settled down to our books again when Sedan's Day, the second of September, arrived, and all the Germans turned out to celebrate the victory over France in 1870.

The Burgdorf green was again occupied with booths and stands of all sorts, while among other contests was one which consisted in two boys, with their hands tied behind their backs, eating their way through a raspberry pie to a twenty mark gold-piece placed in the centre of it ; the one first reaching the money being entitled to keep it. As the pie was an immense one, the task was not by any means easy, while the appearance of the boys' faces during its progress gave rise to shouts of laughter on every side.

Young Albert von Rothstall, my friend of the railway journey, had gone to England shortly after his return to Burgdorf ; but Starleigh and I often took walks in the direction of the Rothstall mansion, a large, rambling sort of building, surrounded by handsomely laid-out grounds and situated at some distance from the town.

And now I began to make acquaintances among the German youth of the place. Indeed with one of them, the son of a Burgdorf magistrate, I became very intimate, and to this day have kept up a lively correspondence with him.

About the first of October a dancing-school was opened, and Starleigh and I remembering how enviously we had regarded Harvey Wintville's proficiency in the art at Baden, determined to attend. So when it was announced that there was to be a private class formed, to consist of eight ladies and an equal number of gentlemen, we made haste to join ourselves to this highly respectable company. We met twice a week and never shall I forget what a sight it was to see the boys on one side and girls on the other, either all sitting primly along the walls or engaged in hopping first on the right foot, then on the left, in the first stages of the course.

Some of the lads were very pleasant, and with one or two I formed quite a friendship.

But at first we dared not so much as speak to the girls, for in Germany the rules of etiquette are so very strict that Starleigh and I often wondered how the young people ever got married, as they seemed to our minds never to have an opportunity of proposing. However, as it would scarcely do for us to dance the waltz with one of our own sex, it was at length announced, after each division had been thoroughly drilled in the steps, in the art of bowing and making a courtesy, and the boys duly exercised in taking off their caps, backing out of the room, and such other accessories to a society education, it was given out after all this preliminary training, that at our next lesson we were to attempt the polka with partners.

This fact caused not a little excitement among the select sixteen, and many a discussion did Starleigh and myself have over the problem which beauty we should respectively choose.

As it turned out, we were not left any choice in the matter, for by reason of our being strangers, we rather hung back when " Take your partners !" was called out, and the result was that we were forced to content ourselves with neither the prettiest nor the most agreeable of the young ladies.

But this first rush for the fairest was as nothing compared to what followed upon a more intimate acquaintance with the Fräuleins. As soon as the dance was announced, there was a general stampede for the other side of the room, and it not infrequently happened that two eager youths would collide on the passage or before the lady.

However, I will not stop to describe all these incidents, nor how we did our best to make ourselves agreeable to our partners, nor the grand ball given at the close of the term. Suffice to add that we both enjoyed it all hugely, and if we did learn a waltz that is danced neither in America nor England, we also learned how to carry on a German conversation.

And so the glorious autumn days went by till the winter holidays drew near. I anticipated much pleasure in passing a Christmas in the Fatherland, a pleasure that was only marred by the fact that my friend Starleigh was to return to England with the new year, his father having made arrangements to place him in a business college at that time.

"But what am I to do here all alone?" I demanded again and again, adding desperately: "I'll go too, then," and perhaps I might have carried this threat into execution, and made this tale a thrilling one by recounting my daring escapade across the English Channel, had not two letters, received just before the holidays, put me in good humor again. One was from my father, stating that he had important news to impart, namely, that he thought it high time I saw some of the life in German cities, and that consequently I was to spend two or three months in Dresden, at a boarding house which had been recommended to him by a friend just returned, there to finish up my study of the language with a celebrated professor whom he named. My departure was fixed for the week after New Year's.

The other letter was from Wintville, who wrote that he and his father expected to reach Dresden some time in January, to remain there till March.

This intelligence, as may be imagined, considerably lessened my grief over Starleigh's departure, although I still continued to think very mournfully of the event. But the twenty-fifth of December was only a week off, and the snow and the ice, so dear to every boy's heart, had come. We brought forth our skates from the depths of our trunks, and enjoyed many a brisk race over the frozen surface of neighboring ponds.

It is the custom of the country for each member of the family, from the head down to the humblest servant, to give a present of some sort, and a pleasant sight it was, when, after tea, on Christmas Eve, the seldom-used parlor was thrown open, displaying to view the small, but brilliantly lighted tree and little tables standing round, each belonging to one person, and all filled with gifts of every value, style, and size. The next morning there was service in the Lutheran Church at six o'clock, and as it was still dark each worshipper carried a candle, which produced a very strange effect when they had accumulated to the number of a hundred or so.

The day thus begun passed off merrily enough, as did the following week of holiday.

These festivities over, Starleigh and I prepared to leave Burgdorf and one another, and on the third of January, after a lonely journey through a snow-storm, I arrived bag and baggage at my new boarding house in Dresden.

CHAPTER X.

I was very much pleased with the capital of Saxony, which reminded me a good deal of Stuttgart ; in fact almost all the German cities appeared alike to me.

When I had been there a week I met Wintville in the street, and after that we were always together. With him I visited the famous picture gallery, the celebrated manufactory of Dresden China, the various museums and collections, and many interesting points around the city.

About the middle of January we had a cold snap, which Harvey and I improved to the fullest extent by skating daily on the small pond in the royal Grosser Garten, which was patronized by a much greater number of Americans and English than Germans. On the occasion of the opening of the handsome new Court Theatre in February, we saw the King and Queen of Saxony riding through the streets in their carriage of state, with two footmen standing behind waving flaming torches in the air.

Yet I will not linger over these Dresden days, although they were among the pleasantest that I spent in Europe ; but will hasten on to Paris and the great

Exposition, whither I was to go in company with Harvey and Mr. Wintville, the latter of whom my father knew in a business way.

This arrangement was very satisfactory to myself, for otherwise I might never have seen the most beautiful city in the world, as it had been at first determined that I was to return to America in April by the steamer on which I came out. According to the new plan, I was to travel with the Wintvilles till they landed in New York, about the first of June, crossing the ocean on one of the English lines.

We left Dresden for Berlin the middle of March, the latter city producing quite a favorable impression on me. The main street, *Unter den Linden*, where the Emperor was twice shot at a few months afterwards, is very pretty, lined as it is with palaces and leading one through handsome archways and over graceful bridges. We took a drive through the Thiergarten, hoping to meet Kaiser Wilhelm, but only succeeded in seeing the Empress Augusta, who was walking along one of the paths in the park, followed at a respectful distance by two footmen. As we passed her our driver took off his hat, as did every one else in the vicinity.

The next day we had a long journey to Cologne, which proved to be the most interesting city I had visited, every thing about the place seeming so odd. The streets are very crooked and narrow, while the odor in some of them affords sufficient reason for the manufacture of the scented water for which the town is famed. The cathedral is grand in the extreme, especially when one looks up at its vast dimensions by night.

In our ride through the city we crossed the Rhine on the bridge of boats, and saw the house of which the following legend is related :

There was once a man who declared he would not believe a certain thing till his horses walked out of their stable, up-stairs to the attic, and there looked out of the window, which they did, as the two heads stuck out from the upper story to this day testify. We refrained, however, from examining them too closely.

We left for Paris at eight o'clock in the evening, and arrived near noon of the following day. We rode in a cab to a large hotel on one of the boulevards, where I got out in a state of the most intense excitement.

What an immense, busy city it was! We had driven through street after street, all lined with stores, all crowded with pedestrians and carriages. I had never believed there were so many omnibuses in the world, and as for cabs, they actually seemed to spring up out of the ground. And yet, notwithstanding all this traffic, the streets were clean and solidly paved, while the sidewalks were broad and ornamented with handsome lamp-posts and queer little round houses, the upper part of glass covered with advertisements, in which were seated old women selling newspapers.

Harvey had been in the city before, and after lunch he took me out to show me the new opera house, which was near by, a magnificent structure, with its tall, marble columns, elegant statuary, and glistening golden harp at the very top. However, as I do not wish to lend to this history any thing of a guide-bookish air, I shall refrain from giving a detailed description of the gay French capital, only mentioning those monuments that struck my fancy the most forcibly, namely, the Arch of Triumph, at the head of the Champs Elysées, and the Tomb of Napoleon I. in the Invalides.

I did not think the Bois du Bologne half so nice as Central Park, and as for the stores and public buildings, there are very few of them that, to my mind, can surpass some of those recently erected in New York. But it is the manner in which Paris is laid out that gives it its chief beauty. There are parks without number, and every few blocks one comes upon a large square, adorned in the centre with a tall, handsome column, commemorating some great event in French history.

The Place de la Concorde, situated at the foot of the Champs Elysées, and where formerly the guillotine performed its horrible task, is now one of the most beautiful spots in the city, while almost all traces of the late war have been removed, if I may except the ruins of the Tuileries Palace.

The weather was mostly fine during our stay, and every afternoon Harvey and I walked up and down the Champs Elysées, which is the nearest approach to a promenade on Fifth Avenue one can find in Europe. Here we either strolled along the pleasantly shaded paths, paid two sous apiece for a chair that we might sit down and watch the carriages, or looked on at the Punch and Judy shows, which are the delight of all the Parisian children, and which can be witnessed almost as well outside the ropes as by paying two cents to go within.

Another of our favorite amusements was roller-skating at the Rink, where there was a smooth floor of asphalt and a fine band of music. We also spent a deal of time atop of the omnibuses, of which the Paris system is well-nigh perfect, as no more than a certain number of passengers are allowed to ride on one vehicle, there being stations scattered all through the city at which tickets, in the shape of numbers, can be procured, entitling the holder to enter in his turn; but if the 'bus be filled before his number is reached he must wait for the next one.

We visited the circus once or twice, where, after the performance, in the course of which the riders received many tumbles that did not seem to disconcert them in the least, the audience was permitted to pass out through the stables, which were adorned with mirrors and brilliantly lighted by crystal chandeliers.

The way they managed things at the theatres, however, struck me as being rather old fashioned, for just before the play was to begin a bell was rung by somebody on the stage (which bell, by the way, sounded exactly as those do that are rung for supper in a country boarding house), and then somebody else pounded three times with a heavy mallet, which was the signal for the curtain to rise, this latter operation being repeated before each act.

But I promised not to enter into detalis, so I will end this chapter right here, and invite my readers to the opening of the great Exposition.

CHAPTER XI.

The first of May had arrived, and notwithstanding that the grounds and buildings still swarmed with gardeners and workmen, the Exhibition was to be thrown open on this, the appointed day.

The ceremonious part of the programme was to be in one sense private, as only those who had received cards of invitation were to be admitted. The only way to procure these precious bits of pasteboard was through the foreign ministers, and Harvey and I were among the unlucky majority that did not obtain any, for our ambassador had been presented by the government with but three hundred tickets to distribute through the American colony, numbering in the neighborhood of a thousand.

However, as it afterward turned out, we did not miss much, as the crowd was so great that nothing could be either seen or heard of the proceedings, during which, as it was later reported, President MacMahon himself was so flurried that he completely upset the most important speech of the inauguration, declaring that "the opening is exposed," instead of "the exposition is open."

Nevertheless, Harvey and I determined to participate so far as we were able in the celebrations of the day, and to that end took a walk down the boulevards in the forenoon in order to see the decorations.

Nearly every house hung out a flag, and many of the buildings were adorned with those of all nations.

Rue de Lafayette presented a particularly striking appearance, for it is the longest straight street in Paris, and looking up it, as we did from its lower end behind the Opéra, it seemed one mass of bunting of all colors.

Fired with enthusiasm by the gay scenes on the avenues, Harvey and I straightway purchased some French and American flags, and unfurled them to the breeze from our two windows at the hotel.

"Now we must take our stand on the Champs Elysées and see the grand procession pass," said my friend after lunch, and away we hurried, as the opening at the Trocadéro was set down for two o'clock sharp.

Well, we waited and waited, while the formerly bright blue sky grew blacker and blacker till, just as we expected the approach of the great cavalcade, the rain came down in such torrents as I never before nor since saw equalled. We had umbrellas of course —for who ever thinks of going out in Paris except during midsummer without one—but the water poured right through them, and such streams came rushing down the sidewalks that we—with all the rest of the crowd that could—were obliged to mount upon the benches placed at intervals along the curbstone, and there we stood, like so many drowned rats, till the storm was over (it only lasted about fifteen minutes).

Then the sun burst forth again in glorious brightness, and shortly afterwards came the procession, consisting of the Marshal President in a superb white carriage with trimmings of crimson, and the Prince of Wales in his equipage of more sombre style, followed by a large troop of cavalry.

These having gone by, we returned to the hotel to change our wet clothes for top-boots and old coats, after which we sallied forth again, to try our luck at obtaining admission to the Exposition grounds.

"Why, everybody's coming back, Harvey," I objected, as crowds upon crowds hurried past us towards the heart of the city.

"There'll be so much the more room for us then," replied this undismayed youth.

We had each purchased a regular ticket that morning, and on arriving at the Trocadéro Palace we presented these at the improvised gates, and were admitted without any hindrance whatsoever. But if we had encountered crowds wending their way homewards, we were now met by as great ones bearing down upon us from every possible direction.

We did not stop to see the sights in the palace, for the simple reason that there was nothing to be seen as yet. Every thing was in an incomplete and very unsatisfactory state, scaffoldings, ladders, carpenters' benches, and chips being the most conspicuous articles in the building.

But when we had passed through this scene of confusion, and stood on the broad piazza that runs all along the inner side of the structure, a very picturesque sight was revealed to us.

Two long, wide flights of steps led down to what was some day to be a garden, but which was now a clinging, inky, mass of mud, being ploughed through by thousands of men and women of all nations. Between the steps was the artificial cascade —over which was situated the stand where the Marshal and his staff had presided at the inauguration— whose waters ran (when they fell, which after the opening was only on Sundays and holidays) into a series of handsome stone basins, ornamented here and there with appropriate groups of statuary.

Harvey and I observed all these objects, and many more besides, as we plunged on through the slush, consoled by the reflection that we were well prepared for the latter; while all the high officials, who had preceded us by an hour or two had been obliged to do so in their best clothes. We crossed the Seine on the Jena bridge—which had been considerably widened for its present use—and after another struggle through clay and crowds, succeeded in gaining the main building on the Champ de Mars.

Here we were properly astounded at the gorgeousness of the Prince of Wales' India collection, kindly loaned by him to occupy the most prominent position in the Exhibition, were filled with wonder at the magnitude of England's show, and finally overcome by our patriotic feelings on entering the American department.

But we had no time to stop, as it was now late and the gates closed at six, so we hurried on through Norway, Sweden, China, Japan—which two latter sections, together with the English, were more nearly complete at that time than any of the others—and then crossed over to the French side, which was not ready at all. Disgusted with the lines upon lines of great cloths covering up almost every thing in the department, we started to leave by one of the side gates.

Here we found more mud than ever, with boards laid down at inconvenient distances apart, thus contributing an edifying spectacle in the way of feats of jumping performed by lightly shod visitors. We had decided to return by one of the Seine boats, and accordingly wended our way along the river bank in the midst of such slush and such a mixed, garlic-reeking crowd as I hope never again to encounter. Thus ended our first visit to the glorious Paris World's Fair of 1878. We had been present on the opening-day, we had borne away with us—on our boots—some of its precious soil, and we were content.

But the celebration of the event was not yet over. In the evening the whole city was to be illuminated, so after dinner Harvey and I once more started out to behold the crowning wonder of the occasion.

"Suppose we ride down to the Bastille and back atop of the omnibus," I suggested, and Harvey agreeing, we walked up the boulevard towards the Madeleine, which was the terminus of the route.

But the further we went, the denser became the crowd, till finally we could do no more than submit to be borne along with it at a snail's pace. The street was blockaded with carriages, and everything seemed to be at a deadlock. The murmur of many voices sounded strangely on the night air, while the glare of thousands of lights threw a deep glow over the whole scene, which was one not soon to be forgotten.

At length we managed to reach the omnibus stand, which was only a few blocks distant, but there were so many people around it that at first we despaired of ever even getting near a 'bus. However, by degrees we squeezed through the crowd, and finally succeeded, by a series of gymnastics, in attaining two seats on top.

But our troubles were not yet over, for we had not gone five feet before we were blocked, in common with all the other vehicles, and compelled to remain in one spot for fifteen minutes at a time. At last the driver was obliged to deviate from his prescribed route and take to the side streets, thus carrying rage and disappointment to our hearts, who had so fondly hoped to have beheld all the flashing glories of the grand boulevards.

But there was still enough to fully occupy our attention, and in crossing the new Avenue de l'Opéra we obtained a fine view of that building, standing out against the sky, one mass of gaslight.

Every thing was illuminated, from the churches with the pipes laid along their eaves down to the most insignificant little shop with its tiny Chinese lantern swinging over the door.

But the most interesting thing of all was the crowd, all the streets seeming alike choked with men, women, and children, for having lighted up his own windows each went out to behold his neighbors'.

"I wonder if their revolutions were any thing like this?" whispered Harvey, as the hoarse murmur of the many voices rose up all around us, the dense mass surged to and fro with excitement, while the heavens reflected back the glow of the great city.

I shuddered a moment as I thought of the guillotine, and then we both forgot the subject in watching the Roman candles and sky-rockets that were constantly shooting up from all sides.

After many delays we reached the Place de la Bastille, and there taking another omnibus, we rode along the famous Rue de Rivoli, up through the Faubourg St. Honoré, and by the Elysée Palace, the Marshal's residence. We did not get back to the hotel till long after midnight, and next morning were very much surprised to learn that there had not been an accident of any kind nor scarcely a disturbance.

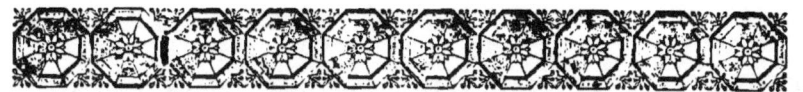

CHAPTER XII.

HARVEY and I paid half a dozen more visits to the Exposition, and although the garden on the Champ de Mars, with its pretty little lake, cunning bridge, artificial rocks, and graceful fountains came to be very attractive in appearance, notwithstanding the Avenue of Nations, where one could take in the peculiarities of each at a glance, and finally in spite of the Prince's Indian loan, Wintville and I were patriotic enough to think that our Centennial was the best of all.

On our last visit—for we were to depart for England the middle of the month—I thought I would note down a few of the most important exhibits, and had just reached the second article when a hand was laid on my shoulder, and a *gendarme* gave me to understand that such things were not allowed.

I now began to look eagerly forward to my return to America after such a long absence, and also anticipated with much pleasure meeting Starleigh in London, where we were to stop for a few days. So in due course our stay in Paris came to an end, and with it my life on the Continent.

We crossed the English Channel at Calais and

Dover, the shortest and roughest passage, and although I was not sick I felt heartily glad when we reached the other side, for the boats are small, with but poor accommodations, and as everybody is generally ill, the scenes on board are not of the most agreeable character.

And now for the first time I set foot on the soil of Great Britain. How queer it sounded to hear the boys talking English, as they fished from the pier at Dover, and how lovely the broad fields, the winding roads, and the green hedges looked, as we sped on to London, the metropolis of the world!

What a great, noisy, smoky city it was, and how funny the 'bus drivers appeared, each wearing a high, beaver hat, and all having the same round, red face! The conductors of the same vehicles stood behind on a bit of a board, holding on by means of a strap which allowed their bodies to swing from side to side in a seemingly most perilous fashion.

Then again I observed, as we rode along in the cab, numbers of smart looking soldiers walking about very proudly in their red coats, and each carrying a small wooden cane, or "stick," as they would call it.

"There's Buckingham Palace!" suddenly exclaimed Harvey, who had been in London before.

I looked in the direction indicated, expecting to behold a magnificent marble mansion, but saw only a great, sombre-colored building standing in a park.

Our hotel, on the other hand, proved to be a very handsome structure, having somewhat the appearance of a church. Here Starleigh, whom I had notified of our arrival, came to see us, and we three passed the time far into the night in talking over our travels and continental life.

The next day we rode on the omnibuses and the penny boats on the Thames, which latter modes of conveyance have no bells, the captain instead calling out, " Start her !" or " Stop her !" to a boy, who in turn screams down the command to the engineer.

We visited Westminster Abbey with its Poets' Corner and tombs of the old kings ; climbed to the top of St. Paul's, and talked to one another in its famous Whispering Gallery ; paid a call on Madame Tussaud, where we several times mistook the wax figures for other visitors, and were hurried through the Tower by one of the officials, who talked so fast that I had as much difficulty in understanding him as the German in Stuttgart. In the latter place the most interesting things, to my mind, were the thumb-screws, and the spot stained with the blood of sovereigns.

The following day Harvey and I rode out in the direction of Greenwich, and saw the naval training-school, with the full-rigged ship standing on the lawn before it. Forty-eight hours afterwards a small steamboat took us and a host of other passengers from the Princess Dock, Liverpool, out to the great black steamer that lay waiting for us in the middle of the Mersey.

As may be imagined, I was in a great state of excitement when the anchor was weighed and the ship started on her voyage to America. Then, as I looked back on the countries I had lived in, and the foreign manners I had observed during the past year, I felt proud of the fact that I had been born across the waters, in the "land of the free and home of the brave."

We reached Queenstown the afternoon of the following day, and spent quite an entertaining half hour in watching the steerage passengers, with their Irish luggage, come on board.

But the next morning, whew, what a storm we met! I thought when I first woke that it would be impossible for me to lift my head from the pillow; but I managed to "weather it," as the sailors say, and enjoyed the remainder of the voyage hugely.

And so my Diary of Foreign Travel ends (it is the very same I came so near losing at Lucerne), and I am no longer Harry Ascott Abroad.

THE END.

www.ingramcontent.com/pod-product-compliance
Lightning Source LLC
Chambersburg PA
CBHW032244080426
42735CB00008B/995